This book is dedicated to my children.

I couldn't give you the material things,

So, I'll just give you the information...,

FIRST TAKE A DEEP BREATH...

OK...So, now you are RICH and you are dreaming about all the things that you could never have done before in your life. It feels good doesn't it?

But, how would it feel if you woke up one day and it was all gone and you were back to square one where you started? Not so good, huh?

Well...that is exactly what can and will happen if you do not understand how rich people **STAY RICH.**

I have always said: **"That it is very easy to get rich...it is very hard to stay rich." (Same thing with getting famous...but that's another book.)**

You could spend a lot of time and a lot of money paying other people to give you advice or trying to learn what you need to know to be a successful millionaire, or you can just read this short booklet.

A successful millionaire is someone who is not only rich, but they know what to do with their money and how to NOT go broke in a short time after getting, earning, or winning it.

I will not be able to give you in depth INVESTMENT advice here. You will definitely still have to go to a broker or Investment Counselor for that. I can however, give you some valuable leads into what types of investment products are available and what you should be looking into as potential additions to your Investment Portfolio.

Everything you do from this point forward will depend on 5 things:

a. Your Age
b. Where You Live
c. Whether You are Married or Single
d. Whether You have Children or Not
e. How Careful, Generous, or Crazy You Are.
        (I will explain that one later)

GET EDUCATED FIRST:
Learn as much as you can about the laws in your particular state regarding **disclosure of your name and address for claiming your Lottery**

prizes. Some states require that you to submit to the media for pictures, etc. and some do not. I, personally would not want anyone to know that I was a millionaire, no less a potential **BILLIONAIRE.**

What to Do If You Win the Lottery

I. Before Claiming Your Prize

Laying a good Fiscal Money foundation is key to making the most of your good fortune. Before you rush out to claim your winnings, you must address the following items first:

A. Protect that ticket and take your time deciding what to do next.

- **First of all, protect your winning lottery ticket.** Make paper copies, store digital copies, invest in a home safe or take the ticket to the bank to store it in a safe deposit box.

- **Once you have your ticket secured,** take your time to contact the lottery authorities. This is for several reasons, but primarily to allow the media hoopla of a big winner to die down and to give yourself time to breathe and plan for your soon-to-be new life.

- **Most lotteries give winners up to 180 or 365 days** to claim their prize, so taking a week off before claiming yours can do a lot for your mental state.

B. Don't Quit Your Job Just Yet Unless You Have at least 6 Months of Savings in the Bank.

- It's what you have always dreamed of: quitting your job to retire to the islands with a cold tropical drink, right? But don't make that decision too fast. You have financial planning to address and you want to be sure you didn't mistake the numbers or the date on your "winning" lottery ticket.

- Just remember to keep your good fortune QUIET at work too. A silent smile is all you need before your boss starts looking for someone to replace you.

C. Hire the Right Professionals

YOU WILL NEED:
A tax attorney
A family planning attorney, and
A licensed accountant.

- When you win a large lottery jackpot, you will need to surround yourself with professionals. Hire yourself a good attorney who is well-versed in financial issues, as well as a solid fee-based financial advisor and a CPA Accountant.

- You are going to need them to help you make the best decisions for your future. Moreover, if you feel uncomfortable about any advice you receive, get a second opinion. You can afford it.

D. Immediately Change Your Address, Disconnect Your Phone and Go Unlisted

- Once word gets out that you've won millions, you are going to hear from a lot of people with their hands out. Charities, causes, friends, long-lost family members, work acquaintances, investment advisors, you name it – you will hear from them all.

- Before claiming your money, change your phone number to a new, unlisted one and get a post office box for your mail. That will make it harder for some of these people to find you.

- **Do not answer your phone and send every call to voice mail if you have to.**

- Learn to be as **INCONSPICUOUS AND LOW KEY** as possible. You will probably want to buy a fancy new car as one of your first purchases. That might not be such a good thing, especially if you live in a high crime area and you haven't moved to your new home yet. You might want to move out of your present home into a local hotel, or extended stay motel until all of the "hooplah" about your win has died down, if possible.

II. Claiming Your Prize

- You can receive your lottery winnings either as a "lump-sum" or as an annual payment spread out over 20 to 30 years. Lottery players used to have to choose between lump sum or long-term payments before paying for their ticket, but a law in 1998 changed it so you can select after you win. There are pros and cons to both choices, so consider each option carefully.

A. Taking the Lump Sum Payment

- When you take a lump sum payout, you won't actually receive the full jackpot amount. The advertised winning jackpot amount is based on the lottery paying you through AN ANNUITY over 20 or 30 years and not all at once.
- So when you take the lump sum, they pay you the current cash value of the jackpot, which is *much less* than each annual payment added up. More often than not, this reduced amount equals *about half* of whatever the winning jackpot amount was. But that doesn't mean the lump sum payment is a bad option.

There are other significant pros and cons as well:

Advantages

- The money could be worth a lot more than the initial payout if carefully and wisely invested.
- Winnings are taxed at current tax rates, which could be higher in the future.
- Older people are guaranteed to get their entire winnings via the lump sum.
- There is no risk of being subject to unknown future variables that can affect your payout.

- **You're guaranteed to at least receive the lump sum.**

Disadvantages

- Poor financial management of a lump sum payment, such as an overly aggressive investment portfolio or careless and outlandish spending, could leave you penniless.
- As mentioned above, that $10 million jackpot lottery ends up being around $5 million in real money and only $3 million (or less) after taxes.
  That is NOT A LOT of money if you need to spread it out over 20 or 30 years.
- You give up a guaranteed income stream.

B. Taking the Long-Term Payout

When you take the long-term payout, you receive the full amount of the jackpot over a period of 20 to 30 years. Here are some of the most important advantages and disadvantages to taking it:

Advantages

- Annual payments provide long-term cash flow.
- An annual payment will likely land you in a lower marginaL INCOME TAX BRACKET than the lump sum, so you may pay less in taxes over the payout term.
- You can't "run through" your entire winnings at once.
- You can better budget and maintain a certain standard of living with a guaranteed annual payment.

Disadvantages

- You lose the opportunity to invest the lump sum and take advantage of compound interest.

- The annual payout is not adjusted for inflation, which means it becomes slightly less valuable every year.

- If you die before payments conclude, the remainder of your winnings may or may not pass to your heirs. This depends on the lottery and the state you won in.
- If the lottery goes out of business, your payments might end, also.
- You have limited access to winnings. For example, if an emergency or opportunity arises, you can't access any more than your annual payment amount.

III. After Claiming Your Prize

OK, so you made the necessary arrangements before asking for your winnings and you decided how you want to be paid. Now what?

- ### A. Talk to the People You Hired

  If you hired the right people, they are there to help, so use them often. If you find that you don't trust them, hire new people. This kind of wealth can be scary if you're not used to it, so seek qualified help and use it to make educated decisions.

- Be especially aware of your new tax bracket and what financial obligations you may have to report you new income to the IRS. Your CPA will give you more information about TAX SHELTERS and how to protect yourself against illegal activities or other litigation.

- ### B. Pay Off Your Debt

  Whether it's leftover student loans, a second mortgage, credit cards, or auto loans, pay off the majority of the debt that you've carried around for years. That being said, you may want to keep your primary mortgage as long as it has a low interest rate. This is because the more money you have, the higher tax bracket you're often in, and the more important tax deductions become.

- Either way, get rid of all your high interest debt, and then consult with your professionals to determine what to do with the rest.

- **C. Start an Emergency Fund**
Even millionaires run into financial problems, sometimes more so than the rest of us! Therefore, setting up a nice-sized emergency fund is one of the smartest things you can do with your winnings or windfall. A good rule of thumb is to set aside enough to pay for at least six months to one year of expenses.

- **D. Put Away Money for Retirement**
Allocate a percentage of your winnings to retirement accounts, such as an IRA ROTH annuity. You don't want to have to go back to work at 80 after being a jackpot winner, do you?

- **E. Setup College Funds**
Do you have kids or want to provide for someone else's kids? Making tax-free gifts OR setting up a TRUST FUND toward a love one's education can be quite rewarding. One option you can look into is the 529 college savings plan.

- **F. Give to Those Less Fortunate**
Whether it's to a church, a charity, or just to a family member facing hard times, consider sharing some of your good fortune. Plus, when you give to a qualified charity, you get to <u>deduct the donation on your taxes</u>!

- **G. Learn to Say No**
Everyone you know and everyone you have never met is going to ask you for money, for both good and bad reasons. You need to learn to say no to most of them until you decide how you want to spend and save your winnings.
- Otherwise, you could end up being broke before you know it.   This may be one of the hardest things you'll have to do. Rest assured, some people will pressure, threaten, or otherwise try to manipulate you to get their way.

- An easy out can be to say you've agreed to discuss everything first with your spouse, or your parents, or your financial counselor. Pick one and use it if someone just won't leave you alone. A soft heart will lead to an empty bank account!

A Final Word about Lottery Winnings

- Winning the lottery can be a dream come true, but only 1 in almost 200 million people actually win the Powerball lottery, for example. While those are some seriously stacked odds, the fact is that some people do eventually win and usually have no idea what to do afterwards.

AT THIS POINT YOU MAY WANT TO GET A LETTER OF CREDIT FROM THE LOTTO COMMISSION AND GO TO YOUR LOCAL BANK OR CREDIT UNION IN ORDER TO TAKE OUT AN EQUITY OR DEBT CONSOLIDATION LOAN.

GET AS MUCH MONEY AS THE BANK IS WILLING TO GIVE YOU SO YOU WILL NOT HAVE TO USE YOUR OWN CASH TO MAKE INITIAL PURCHASES UNTIL YOUR INVESTMENTS KICK IN.

PAY THE LOAN BACK IN INSTALLMENTS UNTIL YOUR OTHER RETURNS COME THROUGH.

****

The "1/3rd Plan"

(Some of this information may be redundant but it bears repeating to get it ingrained in your head.)

FIRST:

A. Break you money down into thirds.

1. Use the first third for your Monthly Living Expenses.

You must set up a BUDGET to understand where your money should go each month in order for you to not **OVERSPEND** or to lose track of where your money is going.

You must pick a level of living (such as $50,000 per year) for whatever returns you can get on your investments and set up a monthly budget of how that money will be spent. Remember it is going to take at least **A YEAR** to get any substantial returns on your money, so you must be prepared to live off of whatever savings you have budgeted for your every day living expenses.

Divide that amount into the 1/3rd you have set a side for your living expenses and that will tell you how many years you can stretch the money.

Adjust your cost of living levels or levels of spending to "fit" into the amount that you have set aside for those expenses.

You may need to continue working or have an alternate means of support if your investments or savings cannot support your chosen lifestyle for the length of time you desire.

A typical budget based on the percentages of your monthly income should look something like this:

ESTIMATED MONTLY FIXED EXPENSES AND BUDGET ALLOCATION
Base Amt. used for calculations is:
$ _____ (Your yearly income or allotment amount.)

Housing............35%   _____

Transportation..... 5%   _____

(gas only)

Debts............... 15%   _____

Tuition/Daycare... 10%   _____

Food.................. 8%   _____

Security Company...10%   _____

Insurances............. 5%   _____

Entertainment........ 2%   _____

Savings and Investment Contributions = (10%) of monthly income   _____

Now take these amounts from above and plug them into the areas below.

Adjust and allow for items that you either have or don't have to include in your personal expenses. For example: If you eat less food or do not go to the movies often you can eliminate or adjust those amounts and use the money for something else.

ACTUAL MONTHLY FIXED EXPENSES

MORTGAGE   _____

FOOD   _____

TELEPHONE (house)   _____

TELEPHONE (Cell Phone)   _____

CAR MAINTENANCE   _____

INSURANCES   _____

CAR NOTE   _____

TUITION/CHILDCARE (ASP's)*_____

UTILITIES (electric, gas, etc.) _____

SECURITY CO.   _____

(* ASP s = After School Programs)

ENTERTAINMENT   _____

(Break this amount down into the following:)

Cable/Internet   _____

Movies (Outside) _____

Movies (Inside) _____

Planned Trips and Other _____

Cash Savings/Investments _____

Types of Investment:_____

Kid's Allowances _____

Total Monthly Fixed Expense _____

THEN:

Pay Down or Pay Off Your Other Debts. If you have high-interest credit card debt, putting your money towards paying it off will likely give you greater returns than any other option. Pay down or pay off those humongous School Loans and save Interest costs. If you cannot afford to PAY OFF your debts, then bring them CURRENT and keep them current to improve your credit rating.

If you pay off your mortgage or buy a new house be sure to get the best deal that you can for the amount of money that you have to spend.
DO NOT hook yourself into a 30 year fixed mortgage on a million dollar mansion if you are over 50 years old. You might regret it when you are 75 or 80 years old, and still have another 5 or 10 years to go to pay off your house.

Remember: Large houses have large maintenance bills. Consider who will clean and maintain the insides and outside of the property. Are you going to hire a crew of servants or not? Do you have management skills to oversee a large crew of people living and/or working in your home? Many a celebrity (MC Hammer, Roseanne and Tom Arnold, Sammy Davis, Jr., and many others) have had to and are presently selling their large mansions; "downsizing" to more manageable houses. A mansion may be your dream home, but the upkeep can and will break your budget if you are not prepared for the extra expenses.

You don't want to have to worry about having a decent place to live when you are 80 years old, with no job and no other means of support. Therefore, a condo or townhouse may be a better option and even a fully furnished nice 2 BR apartment might be a better choice than a big house that needs a lot of care, utilities and maintenance.

Invest in Other Real Estate. It is now a "buyer's market"...which means that there are so many properties available that buyers have the upper hand in making good deals. However, the glut of properties also means that there is A LOT of available inventory and you probably will be able to pick up some bargains in foreclosures or other Government properties. BUT, you must be prepared to pay the mortgages, maintenance, taxes and other expenses to keeping that property on the market until you find a suitable tenant or buyer. So, be very careful what you choose.

2. Use the second third of your money for, Investments, Insurances and Savings.

INVESTMENTS

Nowadays, with all the volatility in the Stock Market, Wall Street might not be the best place for your money to reside. Your investment counselors will give you more detailed advice, but the main thing you need to consider when it comes to most investments is this:

YOUR AGE: plays a major roll in deciding how long you can access your money or how much your money will benefit you in the long run.

YOUR RISK TOLERANCE: Can you afford to take big risks, or are you only able to take advantage of the small ones? (This is called your Investment Horizon.)

YOUR LEVEL OF INVOLVEMENT: Do you want to go full out into stocks, bonds, or other corporate products or do you just want a few non-commercial products?

The cost of a share of stock that is listed on the Dow Jones Stock Reports does not tell you what your initial investment must be in order to purchase that particular stock in that particular company.

Some companies require minimum purchases over $100,000. You may be better off just being a part of a Mutual Fund or an Investment Club with your money, and pool it with other people who want to make money with you.

A few famous investment counselors are saying that your best bets these days are: COMMODITIES like: gold, silver, platinum or other precious metals, jewels and stones. Also look into: new inventions, pharmaceuticals, paper products, "GREEN" products, or other developing business ideas that are coming out.

 ** CAUTION: DO NOT (I repeat) DO NOT WASTE YOUR MONEY ON YOUR CRAZY BROTHER'S OR DEADBEAT UNCLE'S or ANYONE ELSE'S FARFETCHED BUSINESS IDEAS...

Unless you know for sure that it is a really great idea, it has been patented or tried already, or they are already making money with it.
You are not a private "Shark Tank" and you will regret wasting your money like that in the long run.

INSURANCES

Are a valuable and *very necessary* component of your Savings and Investment portfolio. This is where you will provide for your and your family's futures.

Of course you will need:

Life Insurance... with burial and death benefits to your family. You can either set up a burial fund or purchase pre-paid packages from your local funeral director. You decide what you want and do not let them "talk you into" getting something that you don't want or need for you or your family members.

Health Insurance... Depending upon your age(s) to cover accident or illnesses. Most large insurance companies have multiple plans that you can tailor to your needs. You also must have some sort of health insurance coverage when you file your Income Taxes.

Investment Insurance...in order to "hedge your bets" and investment products protect yourself against "downturns" in the Markets. A good hedge fund manager or other investment counselor will give you advice on how to make money in the Stock Market when the market goes down as well as when it goes up.

SAVINGS

Whatever money that you put away for your future will be your "nest egg" or your "fall back" money. This is money that you vow to not touch under any circumstances. You can keep it in a bank, in your mattress, in a safe in your home, or in an offshore or foreign account. It is up to you where you want to keep it. But, I would advise you to purchase a good SAFE with a combination lock and keep copies of the combination and the keys in a secure place...

BUT, NOT INSIDE THE SAFE (DUH!)

a. Fund Your Emergency Savings. Make sure that you have at least 6 -12 months or more of your monthly budgeted amount put into savings so that you will be able to cover your expenses in the case of accident, injury, disability, or any other situation where you are no longer taking home the same amount of money that you normally do, or you are forced to start living off your savings.

b. Save for Retirement. Companies are now urging their employees to invest in Roth IRA accounts through their own investment firms and to not rely on their 401K or other company Retirement Accounts. This is because if a company goes bankrupt they do not have a fiduciary responsibility to pay their workers ALL of their retirement money until after they have re-organized, and you will have to just take the loss.

(Read about what happened when the infamous Bernie Madoff..."made off" with all those people's retirement funds back in 2006-2008.)

Read more about Retirement funds at this website: http://www.goodfinancialcents.com/company-is-going-bankrupt-what-about-my-pension/)

c. Start a College Savings Fund. If you have young children it would be wise to start a savings fund (called a 529 Savings Plan) which will gain interest earnings while your child is preparing for college. If you have older children, invest in TEST PREP classes and courses to prepare them for taking their ENTRANCE EXAMS like the SAT, ACT, GMAT, MCAT, OR LSAT exams.

Investigate college tuitions and fees, and choose

whether you want your child to attend school in your home state or if you want them to go away to school. If they go away, please remind them to keep your family's financial situation a SECRET.

You do not want your child to be making friends based on what kind of car they drive or how much money their parents are worth.

NOW THIS IS WHERE YOU START HAVING FUN!!

3. Use the last third for Miscellaneous Spending, Vacations, etc.!!

This is the **FUN** part of being a millionaire. You get to shop whenever you want to, travel, meet new people and explore things you have never seen or done before.

BUT DO NOT GO CRAZY WITH THE CREDIT CARDS OR CASH PURCHASES...

Make a list of items that you think you might want or need to buy, take inventory of what you already have and donate what you don't want or need to Charity. How many pairs of shoes or mink coats can one person wear? Take into consideration the size of your home (or your new home) and think about the future purchases you might want to make. In other words: "Don't blow it all or spend it all in one place at one time."

LEARN SMART SHOPPING HABITS.

Do not go crazy buying your kids toys because then they will expect more and more and not respect the value of money in the long run.

Teach them self-control as much as you yourself will need to learn to control your spending.

Give your children reasonable allowances based on: their performance in school or whatever chores you have assigned them in the house.

Just because YOU ARE RICH does not mean that THEY ARE RICH. They have to work for their money to learn fiscal responsibility.

Things to be careful of while you're having fun:

1. Do not carry large amounts of cash on your person. Only carry debit or credit cards that can be easily replaced or hard to get your money from. Protect yourself at all ATM's and beware of Identity Thieves at all times. Have separate cash accounts from which you draw your vacation spending money so thieves will not have access to your main accounts.
$200 is the most cash that you will probably need to carry in your pocket(books). Anything more than that is just temptation for thieves or other losses.

2. Do not give your personal information or deposit money to anyone that you do not feel comfortable around or doing business with.

Including: travel agents, travel guides, hotels, motels, vendors or any other business people you may come across in your travels.

Be sure to make reservations well in advance of your travel especially during high travel periods, holidays, etc. in order to be assured of great accommodations.

You won't want to be put into a horrible room or arrive during a bad weather season, or be put into a room with a horrible view because you didn't make your reservations in time.

Money doesn't always get you what you want.

3. Do not leave your valuables in plain site in hotel or motel rooms and do not trust strangers who may want to talk to you about **ANYTHING** in the hotel bars or lounges. Hotels have safes at their front desks that you can use if you do not want to carry your valuables with you. Unsavory characters troll for millionaires just waiting for their next targets, so watch your conversations and be aware of who is watching you or your family members.

4. Find a travel partner or someone who knows the territory, if you do not feel comfortable traveling alone...or, join a travel

club! Do not just go to places that everyone else goes to unless you really want to go there. Try to find "out-of- the-way" or new and exciting places to explore. Take language lessons ahead of time and be sure to learn the customs of the country to which your are going. Be aware of your surroundings at all times.

DO NOT EXPLORE STRANGE PLACES ALONE; especially after dark.

NOW THIS IS WHERE IT GETS REALLY CRAZY...

5. Be sure to give back to the Society and allow 10% for tithes to your local church or charity.
Giving is as important as receiving and you will appreciate your wealth when you give some back to friends and family. But, don't fall victim to the "gimme- gimme" syndrome where you constantly give more than you can afford to your family or strange charities that send you solicitations.

Especially, DO NOT give large amounts to your church or church members thinking that they will use the money wisely or build a memorial in your honor. Chances are the money will get wasted and they will come back to you with their hands out time and time again.

Learn to say: "**No...I can't do that...**" and control your spending habits or else you will end up broke and bitter--- if you don't learn your wise money lessons.

A FINAL WORD ABOUT UNWANTED LITIGATION AND LAW SUITS

Your legal advisor can give you more information about how to avoid lawsuits or how to avoid people who may wish to lay claim to your money for whatever reason. Just be very careful bout whom you choose to befriend or hire. **People are just waiting for you to make a mistake or make up a reason, so they can take you to court for your money.** There is no way to avoid divorces or separation agreements between spouses and these laws depend upon the state in which you live.

Check your state laws carefully for regulations involving **COMMUNITY ASSETS** and what you must do in the case of legal claims against you in your local **FAMILY OR ESTATE** courts.
Your lawyer or other legal advisor can give you more information.

GOOD LUCK AND GOD BLESS YOU!

PLEASE STAY SAFE AND USE YOUR MONEY
WISELY
FOR THE GOOD OF HUMANITY AND NOT
JUST FOR YOURSELF!

FIVE STEPS TO SUCCESS
by Carla Miller-Camacho

1. LEARN TO BE CONSERVATIVE... Truly successful people are not "flashy." Millionaires shop at Sears and other discount stores. That is because you don't get rich by *spending money.* You get rich by **saving and investing money** in things of value.

2. LEARN TO DEFER YOUR DESIRES... Don't succumb to your *immediate desires* at the expense of your *future stability.* Current fashion goes out of style quickly. Invest in CLASSIC items that will last indefinitely.

3. LEARN TO C.Y. A. ...Cover Your Assets. Protect your money and protect your investments with insurance and security. Don't let your hard earned investments be wasted with careless actions.

4. LEARN TO INVESTIGATE... Never listen to ALL of the people who want to tell you what to do with YOUR money. Remember **BERNIE MADOFF...**who "made off" with all those people's money who trusted him because they didn't know what they were doing.

5. LEARN WHEN TO SAY "NO" AND WHEN TO SAY "YES"... Say "no" to things that will **subtract** from your security. Say "yes" to things that will **add** to your security. Never "give in" to the desires of other people that do not and cannot benefit yourself directly.

READ....get Educated
INVESTIGATE...be Curious
ASK QUESTIONS...be Skeptical
and LEARN YOUR LIMITS...Know Yourself!

Made in the USA
Middletown, DE
29 March 2021